butterfly

butter

Markings.

Head of Blind-worm. 1/2

A Book-scorpion
(*Chelifer can-croides*). 5/1

Click-beetle,
natural size.

Sinea diadema, one
of the *Reduviidæ*.
(Line shows natural
size.)

Proxys punctulatus.

Hellgrammite (*a*)
and Hellgrammite-fly.

The Bait-bug.

Parasite of the Beaver (*Platy-psyllus castoris*). (Line shows
natural size.)

Rose-beetle (*Cetonia aurata*).
Vertical line shows natural size.

Agonoderus dorsalis (Le Conte).
Vertical line shows natural size.

The Twig-gir-dler (*Oncideres
cingulata*). 1/1
a, a branch girdled by the beetle.

Hawthorn-tingis
arcuata), one of
enlarged about ten

Flour-beetle (
litor). (Line
size.)

Snowy Tree-cricket (*Œcanthus niveus*).
a, male, dorsal view ; *b*, female, lateral view.

A Species of *Phrynus*, about life-size.

Apple-sl...
pulla...
s, siphon...
cul...

Spiderwort Owlet-moth (*Prodenia flavimedia*).
a, larva ; *b*, wings of moth.

Ground-beetle (*Caloso ...lidum*), natural size.

Eurygaster alternatus; wings partly open. (Line shows natural size.)

Thighed Metapodius (*Metapodius femoratus*).

The C... stem...
a, lar... ting i... ver = st... the bee...

The Cucujo.

...phemeridæ.
...opean May=fly (*Eph...lgata*) and its sub-...va.

Bombardier-beetle (*Brachinus stygicornis*). (Vertical line shows natural size.)

Podisus placidus.
a, enlarged ; *b*, natural size.

Hom...
Tail of a... ing homo... dal verte... dal rays;... bones; *p*,... esses of c... united to... for the so... ral spines...

np

Libellulidæ.
Development of a dragon=fly, showing the subaquatic larva, ...mergence from the pupa, and ...he adult fully winged insect.

A Flea (*Pulex irritans*).
a, puncturing stylets of the proboscis.

A Bristletail (*Lepisma saccharina*). $^{5}/_{1}$

...hymata erosa.

Atypus sulzeri. (Vertical line shows natural size.)

Bacon-beet'e.

One of th... on...

Grape-vine Fidia (*F. viticida*). (Line sh ws natural size.)

fly

by

Ting Morris

· · · · · · · · · ·

illustrated by

Desiderio Sanzi

designed by

Deb Miner

W

FRANKLIN WATTS

LONDON·SYDNEY

Sit very still and close your eyes.

Now open them! **A beautiful butterfly has come to visit your garden.** Watch it flitting about from flower to flower.

Can you see its wings shimmering with bright colours?

Amazingly, your visitor didn't always have wings. Did you know that it was once a creepy-crawly caterpillar? **Turn the page and take a closer look.**

This handsome butterfly with white spots and bright red stripes is called a red admiral. Like all butterflies, it doesn't like the cold. Some red admirals go on long journeys to spend the winter in a warmer place. This butterfly has just come back to enjoy the summer sunshine and to drink from its favourite flowers. But what can it be looking for among the stinging nettles?

ON A WING

You can recognize different kinds of butterflies by the colours on their wings. All red admirals have big red stripes on their front wings. The coloured patterns on butterfly wings are made up of tiny, flat scales. They overlap like tiles on a roof and will rub off if you touch them.

WATCH AND ENJOY!

Don't catch butterflies! You can enjoy watching them in your garden or in the park.

WHAT ARE BUTTERFLIES?

Butterflies are insects. There are thousands of different kinds, and they live almost everywhere in the world. Some butterflies sleep through the winter, and others fly to a warm climate. They feed on the sweet nectar made by flowers.

HOW LONG DO BUTTERFLIES LIVE?

Some butterflies live only for a few days. Others can live for 18 months, but most of that time may be spent in winter sleep.

GIANT SULPHUR BUTTERFLY

INDIAN LEAF BUTTERFLY

ADONIS BLUE BUTTERFLY

COMMA BUTTERFLY

PEACOCK BUTTERFLY

7

The butterfly is searching for a plant on which to lay her eggs, and she must make sure that she finds the right kind. She knows that her young will eat only nettles. If she lays the eggs on another plant, they will starve.

She sniffs the nettle leaves with her feelers and tastes them with her feet. **Then she pushes the eggs out of her body and glues them one by one to the leaves.**

Can you spot them?

EGGS GALORE

Butterfly eggs are tiny and come in all shapes and colours. Some look like pearls and others may have grooves or spikes. A hard shell protects the caterpillar growing inside. The yolk is its food.

The cabbage white butterfly will lay hundreds of eggs on cabbage leaves.

Gulf fritillary eggs are bright yellow at first but soon darken.

The European map butterfly lays a string of eggs.

EGG INTO CATERPILLAR

Most female butterflies lay between 100 and 1,000 eggs. Some will stick rows of 20 to 50 eggs on different leaves and stems with a glue they make in their body. They then fly away and leave the eggs to hatch on their own. Birds, spiders and other animals will eat the eggs if they find them. Out of every 100 eggs laid, only two or three will grow into butterflies.

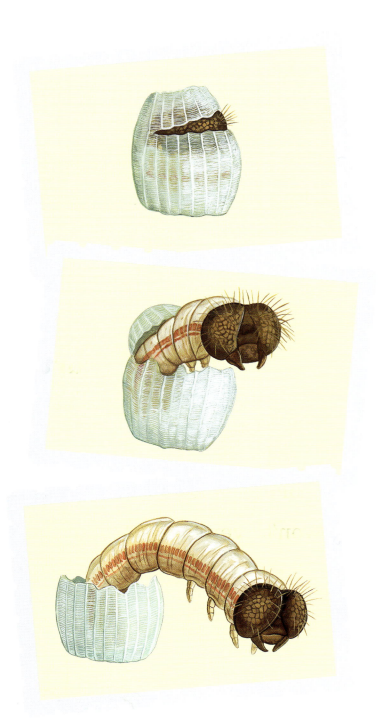

COMING OUT

1 The red admiral caterpillar is hatching. It cuts a round hole in the hard eggshell.

2 The caterpillar wriggles out. A lot of muscle power is needed!

3 Out at last! This is a very dangerous time for a tiny caterpillar.

Inside each egg, a tiny caterpillar is growing bigger and bigger. Five days have passed since the eggs were laid, and some have turned grey. There's not much room inside for a growing caterpillar, so it's time to leave the egg. The caterpillar chews a hole in the shell and wriggles free. **Caterpillars are always hungry, and this one starts to eat at once.** Its first meal is the eggshell.

Another black head pokes out of its shell. Soon there will be lots of caterpillars crawling over the nettles. But they won't ever see their mother. She flew away long ago. These little caterpillars will have to look after themselves.

The eggshell is full of nutrients. After its first meal, the caterpillar is strong enough to look for other food.

11

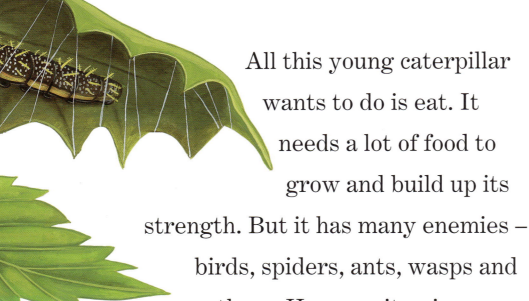

All this young caterpillar wants to do is eat. It needs a lot of food to grow and build up its strength. But it has many enemies – birds, spiders, ants, wasps and others. How can it enjoy a peaceful meal when it could be eaten itself?

The caterpillar builds itself a hide-out. It folds a leaf and glues it together with silk threads. It now has its own little tent, where it can hide until it's safe to crawl out ... and eat and eat and eat.

The forest queen has frightening horns and strange spots.

Monarch caterpillars taste horrible.

Stay away from this spiny small postman caterpillar!

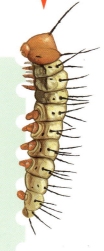

BETTER SAFE THAN SORRY

Caterpillars are a great delicacy for insect-eating creatures. That's why they have to protect themselves. Many hide during the day and come out only after dark for an all-night feast. Most are the same colour as their food plant and so they can hide in the leaves. Some look like twigs and stiffen up when they are in danger. Some caterpillars have prickly hairs and poisonous spikes, which make them unpleasant to eat. Caterpillars may also have startling colours, bright spots, or scary false eyes to frighten their enemies away.

Young swallowtail caterpillars look like bird droppings, so birds leave them alone.

This tiger swallowtail caterpillar is as green as the willow leaves it eats. Look at its scary eyespots.

13

At night, the hungry caterpillar comes out for a good meal. It's getting fatter and fatter. It crawls from leaf to leaf, nibbling as it goes.

Clinging to the nettle stem with its stumpy back legs, the caterpillar uses its front legs to push leaves into its mouth. Its skin feels very tight now, but it won't stretch. Luckily, a new skin is growing underneath, and soon it's time to get out of the old one.

A CATERPILLAR'S BODY

A caterpillar's body is made up of 14 SEGMENTS, or parts. It has eight pairs of legs.

The first segment is the hard, round HEAD, with a mouth and six tiny EYES on each side. The eyes can see only light and dark – not colours.

On each of the next three segments there are two short, flexible legs with sharp claws. These are called TRUE LEGS.

On the next 10 segments there are 5 pairs of stumpy legs called PROLEGS.

ANTENNAE

HEAD

EYES

SPINNERET

TRUE LEGS

PROLEGS

SEGMENT

SUCKERS

At the end of each proleg there is a ring of hooks. On the last segment, a pair of soft stumps work like suckers to hold on to flat surfaces. These different types of legs help the caterpillar cling to plants and move about.

15

After three weeks of eating and four new skins, the caterpillar splits its skin again. It climbs out of the tight old skin and waits for the fresh skin to harden. Soon it's starving again and must make up for missed meals.

With its scary-looking spines, the caterpillar risks another morning snack and continues munching until its skin feels tight again.

Now the caterpillar won't grow any bigger. What do you think will happen next?

TIGHT FIT

When its skin becomes too tight, a caterpillar changes it for a looser fit. It moults, or sheds its skin, by simply crawling out of it. A new skin grows underneath. Most caterpillars moult four or five times.

GREEDY

Caterpillars use their strong jaws to tear off bits of plants and chew them up. They can damage gardens and farmers' crops. These caterpillars are stripping a cabbage.

TRICK OR TREAT

Some caterpillars trick their ant enemies. The caterpillars make a sweet liquid that ants like. So the ants take them to their nest, where they look after them.

17

The greedy caterpillar suddenly stops eating and searches for a good, strong leaf. **There it spins a pad of silk and sews up the leaf.** It grips the pad with the hooks on its tail legs and holds on to the silk thread. Then it hangs upside-down, hidden in the spun leaves.

For the last time, the caterpillar shrugs off its old skin. Underneath there is a hard case that shimmers like gold. This is the chrysalis. Inside, the caterpillar is changing.

SAFE CHANGING ROOMS

A chrysalis cannot defend itself. That's why the caterpillar must look for a safe place – such as the underside of leaves or a garden shed – where it can change. The chrysalis looks brown and wrinkled like an old leaf.

FROM CATERPILLAR TO CHRYSALIS

1 The swallowtail caterpillar attaches a pad of silk to a strong stem and hooks on to it. It bends its head back and spins a silk safety belt around itself.

2 The caterpillar is held by the silk thread. It turns into a chrysalis, or pupa.

3 After a few hours, the chrysalis hardens. The chrysalis does not move or eat, but great changes are taking place inside. These changes usually take two or three weeks, but the swallowtail butterfly stays inside its hard case throughout the winter.

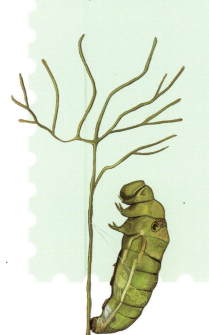

A new butterfly is born on this hot, sunny day. **It has just wriggled out of its chrysalis and can stretch its new wings at last.** But its wings are still soft and wet and crumpled.

The butterfly clings to its old skin – it can't fly yet. It spreads out its wings and warms them in the sunshine. Soon they will be hard and strong, and then this red admiral will be ready for the biggest moment of its life – its first flight!

20

A BUTTERFLY'S BODY

A butterfly's body has three parts – the HEAD, the THORAX, and the ABDOMEN.

On each side of the head is a COMPOUND EYE. It is made up of thousands of tiny lenses, so butterflies can see all around them.

A butterfly uses its ANTENNAE, or feelers, to smell.

It sucks nectar through a long, hollow PROBOSCIS, or tongue, which it keeps curled up when it's not in use.

Butterflies have six LEGS and two pairs of WINGS. The VEINS in the wings are filled with air and help to hold them up.

Butterflies breathe through tiny holes called SPIRACLES. The spiracles are along the sides of the abdomen.

Female butterflies make eggs in their abdomen.

FRONT WING

VEINS

ANTENNAE

BACK WING

EYE

HEAD

PROBOSCIS

LEGS

THORAX

ABDOMEN

The new red admiral flaps its bright wings and glides over parks and gardens, from blossom to blossom. The butterfly unrolls its long tongue, pushes it deep into the flowers, and sucks up the sweet nectar. When it gets dark, it folds its wings and rests among the leaves, so its enemies can't see it. **This purple bush is a favourite meeting place for butterflies, and the red admiral has found a mate.** Look, they are dancing in the air, high above the purple spikes.

SHORT LIFESPAN

Many butterflies live only for a few days. After mating and laying their eggs, they die.

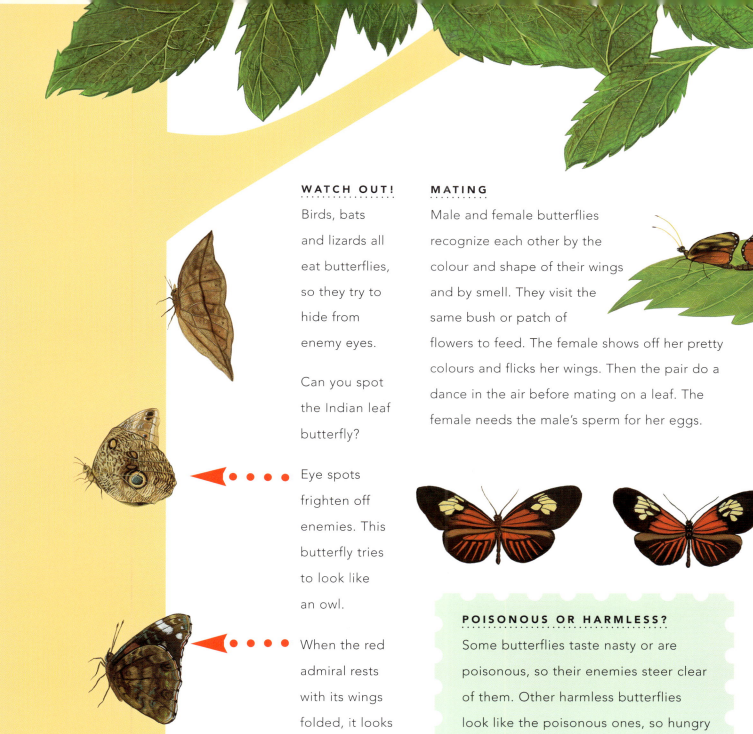

WATCH OUT!

Birds, bats and lizards all eat butterflies, so they try to hide from enemy eyes.

Can you spot the Indian leaf butterfly?

Eye spots frighten off enemies. This butterfly tries to look like an owl.

When the red admiral rests with its wings folded, it looks like part of the tree's bark.

MATING

Male and female butterflies recognize each other by the colour and shape of their wings and by smell. They visit the same bush or patch of flowers to feed. The female shows off her pretty colours and flicks her wings. Then the pair do a dance in the air before mating on a leaf. The female needs the male's sperm for her eggs.

POISONOUS OR HARMLESS?

Some butterflies taste nasty or are poisonous, so their enemies steer clear of them. Other harmless butterflies look like the poisonous ones, so hungry birds leave them alone too.

23

The days are getting shorter, and there's a chill in the air. **Luckily, the red admiral has found an orchard full of ripe fruit, so there's a treat of apple juice to give it extra strength.**

Butterflies can't fly about in cold weather. Some find a sheltered place to sleep through the winter months, but red admirals are strong flyers and they head south for the winter.

Keep an eye on that patch of stinging nettles. If you're lucky, you might see a new family of red admirals there next year.

LONG-DISTANCE CHAMPIONS

Each autumn, swarms of North American monarch butterflies fly thousands of kilometres south to California, Florida and Mexico.

BIG AND BEAUTIFUL

The largest butterfly in the world is the Queen Alexandra's birdwing. Its wingspan measures up to 30 centimetres across.

SUMMER GUESTS

Painted lady butterflies leave North Africa in the spring and fly more than 6,000 kilometres north. They reach Europe in early summer.

FOR REAL

Butterflies come in many shapes and sizes. These pictures show you how big some of them are in real life.

PYGMY BLUE   SMALL COPPER   ZEBRA SWALLOWTAIL

25

QUEEN ALEXANDRA'S BIRDWING

The female butterfly
lays eggs.

Butterfly

Male and
female
butterflies
mate.

A butterfly emerges
from the hard case.

A caterpillar hatches
from the egg.

The caterpillar
eats and
grows.

CIRCLE OF LIFE

After moulting many
times, the caterpillar
becomes a chrysalis.

27

chrysalis The hard outer case that protects a caterpillar while it grows into a pupa. The word can also be used for the pupa itself.

compound eye An eye made up of thousands of tiny lenses.

eyespots Round markings on a butterfly's wings that look like eyes.

lenses Transparent structures that focus light in eyes.

nectar A sweet, sugary liquid produced by flowers.

nutrients Substances in food that are nutritious and provide nourishment.

orchard A field of fruit trees.

proboscis A long, flexible tube that acts like a tongue. A butterfly sucks nectar through it.

prolegs The stumpy legs on the rear segments of a caterpillar.

pupa A young butterfly at the resting stage between a caterpillar and an adult.

scales The thin, flat structures that cover the wings of butterflies and moths.

segments The many parts into which something is divided.

sperm Fluid produced by male animals that makes a female's eggs grow into young.

spinneret The organ in a caterpillar that produces silk threads.

veins Hollow tubes that form the framework of a butterfly's wing.

 An Appleseed Editions book

First published in 2004 by Franklin Watts
96 Leonard Street, London, EC2A 4XD

Franklin Watts Australia
45–51 Huntley Street, Alexandria, NSW 2015

© 2004 Appleseed Editions

Created by Appleseed Editions Ltd,
Well House, Friars Hill, Guestling, East Sussex, TN35 4ET

Illustrator: Desiderio Sanzi

Designer: Deb Miner

ISBN 0 7496 5703 0

A CIP catalogue for this book is available from the British Library.

Printed and bound in the USA

Markings.

ruonis). 4/1   *nalis).* 5/1

natural size.

Head of Blind-worm. 1/2

A Book=scorpion (*Chelifer can-croides*). 5/1

Click-beetle, natural size.

Sinea diadema, one of the *Reduviidæ*. (Line shows natural size.)

Cotton=stainer

a

b

Epeiridæ.
a, male, and *b*, fe-male, of *Epeira stel-lata; c*, characteristic orb=web of an epeirid (*Epeira strix*).

Proxys punctulatus.

a

Hellgrammite (*a*) and Hellgrammite-fly.

The Bait=bug.

Parasite of the Beaver (*Platy-psyllus castoris*). (Line shows natural size.)

Rose-beetle (*Cetonia aurata*). Vertical line shows natural size.

Agonoderus dorsalis (Le Conte). Vertical line shows natural size.

The Twig=gir-dler (*Oncideres cingulata*). 1/1
a, a branch girdled by the beetle.

The
Drag
(*Dro
eatus*

Hawthorn-tingis (*arcuata*), one of the enlarged about ten t

Flour-beetle (*Te litor*). (Line sho size.)

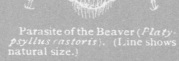
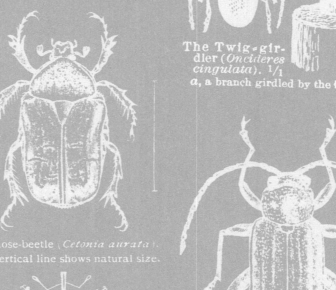
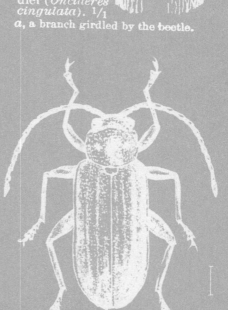

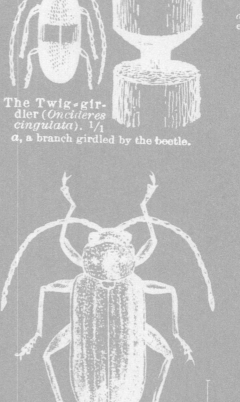

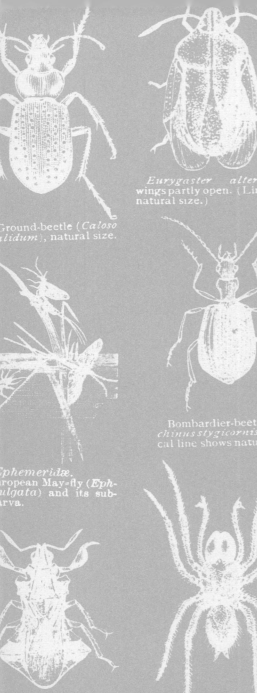

Ground-beetle (*Caloso ...lidum*), natural size.

Ephemeridæ.
...ropean May-fly (*Eph... ...ulgata*) and its sub-
...arva.

Phymata erosa.

Eurygaster alternatus; wings partly open. (Line shows natural size.)

Bombardier-beetle (*Bra-chinus stygicornis*). (Verti-cal line shows natural size.)

Atypus sulzeri. (Vertical line shows natural size.)

A Species of *Phrynus*, about life-size.

Thighed Metapodius (*Metapo-dius femoratus*).

Libellulidæ.
Development of a dragon-fly, showing the subaquatic larva, emergence from the pupa, and the adult fully winged insect.

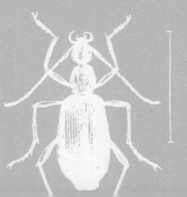

Grape-vine Fidia (*F. viticida*). (Line sh ws natural size.)

a, male, dorsal view; *b*, female, lateral view.

Spiderwort Owlet-moth (*Prodenia flavimedia*). *a*, larva; *b*, wings of moth.

Podisus placidus.
a, enlarged; *b*, natural size.

A Flea (*Pulex irri-tans*).
a, puncturing stylets of the proboscis.

The Cucujo.

A Bristletail (*Lepisma sac-charina*). ⁵/₁

Bacon-beet'e.

Apple-s...
pulle...
s, siphon...

The ... stem ...
a, lar... ting ... ver... the be...

Hon...
Tail of ... ing home... dal verte... dal rays... bones; ... esses of ... united to ... for the a... ral spine...

One of t...

A D...